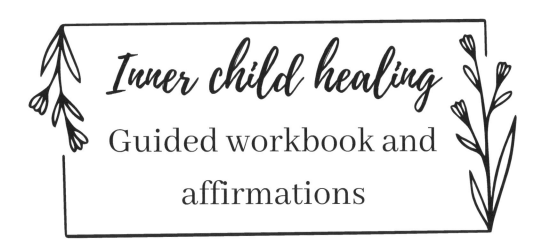

Inner child healing

Guided workbook and affirmations

Inner child healing

This workbook is designed to help you work through both the positive and more challenging aspects of your childhood experience. The aim of this is to ultimately become a happier, healthier person. The prompts are designed to help you identify and magnify the positive, and work through and put to rest the more challenging experiences.

Throughout this journal you will see phrases such as "in your childhood", if it is more helpful to you to choose certain ages rather than your childhood as a whole then you should practice whichever method suits you best.

As facing our childhood experiences can be difficult, take your time, practice self care, and if necessary seek the advice of a professional.

Relationships with others

1. A prominent memory I have of my mother from my childhood is... (if there are no prominent memories, then the main emotion you associate with your mother may be used in its place). Why do I think this memory has stuck with me?

_____

_____

_____

_____

_____

2. What was the relationship between me and my mother like while I was a child? In what ways would I have liked it to be different?

_____

_____

_____

_____

_____

3. If I could go back to ages 5/10/15 (or any other more appropriate age for your experiences), what would I say to my mother now that I have had time to reflect since childhood?

_____

_____

_____

_____

_____

_____

4. A prominent memory I have of my father from my childhood is... (if there are no prominent memories, then the main emotion you associate with your father may be used in its place). Why do I think this memory has stuck with me?

_____

_____

_____

_____

_____

5. What was the relationship between me and my father like while I was a child? In what ways would I have liked it to be different?

_____

_____

_____

_____

_____

6. If I could go back to ages 5/10/15 (or any other more appropriate age for your experiences), what would I say to my father now that I have had time to reflect since childhood?

_____

_____

_____

_____

_____

7. In what ways did my family affect my beliefs about myself?

_____

_____

_____

_____

_____

_____

8. Which of those beliefs are harmful, and how can I challenge them?

_____

_____

_____

_____

_____

9. Which of those beliefs are beneficial, and how can I nurture them?

_____

_____

_____

_____

_____

_____

10. In what ways did my family affect my beliefs about others?

_____

_____

_____

_____

_____

11. Which of those beliefs are harmful, and how can I challenge them?

_____

_____

_____

_____

_____

_____

12. Which of those beliefs are beneficial, and how can I nurture them?

_____

_____

_____

_____

_____

13. What experiences with others in my peer group are prominent memories for me? What is it about these experiences that I keep coming back to? What did I learn from them?

_____

_____

_____

_____

_____

14. How did I think my peers perceived me in my childhood? how did this affect my perception of myself?

_____

_____

_____

_____

_____

15. Who from my childhood made a lasting impression on me and why?

_____

_____

_____

_____

_____

_____

16. For those who made a positive lasting impression on me, can I recognise any of those same traits in myself? Can I amplify those characteristics in myself?

_____

_____

_____

_____

_____

17. For those who made a negative lasting impression on me, how did they affect me? How can I challenge the impact they had on me?

_____

_____

_____

_____

_____

_____

18. When I think back to the authority figures of my childhood (e.g., guardians, teachers, doctors etc), I feel...

_____

_____

_____

_____

_____

19. Where there any of those authority figures that I looked up to? why?

_____

_____

_____

_____

_____

20. How have those figures shaped my behaviour and beliefs today?

_____

_____

_____

_____

_____

21. Where there any of those authority figures that I disliked? Why?

_____

_____

_____

_____

_____

_____

22. How have those figures shaped my behaviour and beliefs today?

_____

_____

_____

_____

_____

23. Are there any people from my childhood I remember being excited or pleased to see? What was it about these people that I enjoyed?

_____

_____

_____

_____

_____

_____

24. Are there any people from my childhood I remember not wanting to interact with, whose company I disliked? What was it about these people that I disliked?

_____

_____

_____

_____

_____

25. Is there anyone from my childhood I wish I still had contact with, or in contrast, anyone I wish I had left behind? why? Can I act on this now?

_____

_____

_____

_____

_____

_____

_____

_____

_____

_____

Happiness and play

26. Who in my childhood did I enjoy spending time with? What qualities in them made them good company?

_____

_____

_____

_____

_____

27. Reflecting on the last prompt, who in my life brings that same kind of enjoyment, or who has similar enjoyable qualities? How can I spend more time with people I enjoy?

_____

_____

_____

_____

28. When I was a child, did I prefer to spend my time alone or with others? Is my answer dependent on other factors? What is it about my own company or the company of others that made it preferable and how can I apply this knowledge to my life now?

_____

_____

_____

_____

_____

_____

29. Continuing this, when I was a child, how did I feel about solo play activities? Some people consider time alone to be time to recharge, others find it under stimulating. Either answer is ok. Do I make time for myself now? If I find alone time under stimulating, then do I still ensure my self-care needs are met in other ways?

_____

_____

_____

_____

_____

30. In contrast, when I was a child, how did I feel about group play activities? Did I find socialisation to be enjoyable? Or did I find a lack of control to be stressful or overwhelming? How has this impacted how I socialise now; do I prefer one-on-one or large group activities?

_____

_____

_____

_____

_____

31. On the whole, what kind of activities brought me joy as a child? list any that come to mind (e.g. reading, television, dancing, being in the garden, tag, hide and seek, walking the dog, etc)

_____

_____

_____

_____

_____

32. Based on my previous answers on, how can I amplify this kind of enjoyment in my present day life? Can I make time to enjoy solo tasks such as reading more frequently? Can I organise more time spent with friends? If I have a busy schedule, can I spare ten minutes to read in the mornings or can I organise a gathering with friends via zoom/skype etc? Are there any classes near me I could join? e.g., dancing, drama, dog walking groups, etc

_____

_____

_____

_____

_____

33. What brought me comfort as a child? E.g., family members, stuffed animals, a favourite film

_____

_____

_____

_____

_____

34. What brings me comfort now? Are there any similarities to what brought me comfort as a child? Do I think I would benefit from reimplementing some of my childhood comforts? (e.g., turning to loved ones with problems not only comforts you but strengthens your bond, watching a favourite film is comforting and can also make nice evening plans). Are any of my comforts harmful to me? How can I challenge them? (e.g., common problems in this area would include overeating or substance abuse, seeking further help from a professional would be a good step in challenging it. It may be useful to think of your other comforts to use as alternatives).

_____

_____

_____

_____

_____

_____

_____

_____

35. In what ways have I carried forward the joys from my childhood into my adulthood? What do I do now that I have always enjoyed doing?

_____

_____

_____

_____

_____

36. what does happiness mean to you?

_____

_____

_____

_____

37. When I think of being happy as a child, I imagine...

_____

_____

_____

_____

_____

38. Does the prior prompt make me wish to change anything in my present life to better align with the image I had in mind? If so, what?

_____

_____

_____

_____

39. What qualities did I have, or did I not have, that made it easier to enjoy myself in my childhood? For example, was I more carefree, less stressed, more energetic, less jaded?

_____

_____

_____

_____

_____

40. Is there a way I can realign myself with these qualities? If I was less stressed, can I find a way to stay calm, can I meditate or create plans/schedules/targets to take the pressure off? If I was more energetic, can I practice spending energy in a healthy way to keep my energy levels up, or practice yoga or stretching to prevent injuries, or maintain a healthy diet to keep energy levels up? Etc.

_____

_____

_____

_____

_____

41. How did my recreational activities change between the age ranges of 5-15? What similarities and differences are there? Think about solo verses group play, and specific activities, perhaps you kept a hobby during this time or perhaps your interests changed entirely.

_____

_____

_____

_____

_____

42. Considering your answer to the last prompt, what external factors impacted those activities? (Your friend groups? The influence of family? The availability of classes?) In an ideal world, would those influences have made a difference? Did you benefit from those external factors or not?

_____

_____

_____

_____

_____

43. Did I enjoy school at any age of my childhood? What aspects of school did I enjoy? (e.g., my peers, favourite subjects, favourite teachers, being out of the home/feeling safe)

_____

_____

_____

_____

_____

44. Did I enjoy any aspects of being at home during my childhood? What aspects did I enjoy? (e.g., being away from peers or other adults/feeling safe, family, pets, my room/toys/books/games, etc.)

_____

_____

_____

_____

_____

45. In what ways can I recreate my enjoyment of my environment now, as an adult? What can I do at home or work to make it a more pleasant and enjoyable place to be?

_____

_____

_____

_____

_____

46. What can I do to ensure my home feels like a safe space as I branch out to try and reignite feelings of childhood joy? It can be as simple as closing the curtains if you have nosy neighbours, or ensuring you have a comforting blanket during a movie night. There are no wrong answers, just think about what makes you feel safe and comfortable.

_____

_____

_____

_____

_____

47. What can I do to ensure I feel safe when I venture out of my home to try my joyful activities? Perhaps group activities will provide a sense of security for example.

_____

_____

_____

_____

_____

48. What coping mechanisms can I turn to if I don't get a positive reaction from one of my activities or if I feel upset or unsafe as I go forward? E.g., grounding techniques, calling a friend, etc.

_____

_____

_____

_____

49. Activities ideas: based on the above prompts in this section, what might I like to try implementing into my life more to encourage a feeling of enjoyment?

_____

_____

_____

_____

_____

50. Action plan: How can I take my ideas from the prior prompt and bring them into action? Take this time to make more solid plans, times, dates, research classes, make time in your diary, etc.

_____

_____

_____

_____

_____

Negative emotions and experiences

51. When I was young, what did I do to calm down after periods of high stress, upset or anger? What were my coping mechanisms?

_____

_____

_____

_____

_____

52. Do I still use these coping mechanisms? If I have changed them, are my current methods more/less effective than my childhood methods? Should I try to reimplement my old methods?

_____

_____

_____

_____

_____

53. When I was young, what were the regular things causing me distress in my life? Was it people, places, activities?

_____

_____

_____

_____

_____

54. Have I been able to remove those stressors from my life now? If not, why? If I cannot remove them then how can I minimise the upset that they cause me?

_____

_____

_____

_____

55. Do I have any feelings of guilt or shame when I reflect on unpleasant childhood experiences? Why? Where did these feelings come from?

_____

_____

_____

_____

_____

56. Take a moment to acknowledge that guilt and shame do not serve you here. You were a child, you deserved to feel safe and happy. You could alleviate some of these feelings by acknowledging the responsibility of those situations was with the adults. Try making statements such as: "I do not need to feel guilty about (event), because (adult) was responsible for checking on us / for keeping me safe". You can get more specific depending on the events that come to mind.

_____

_____

_____

_____

_____

57. Can I forgive myself for whatever I feel guilty or ashamed about? Children should not be made responsible for the safety or emotions of themselves or others, they are still learning about the world they live in. Try to forgive yourself for any involvement in events you hold a negative emotion towards with similar statements as last time.

_____

_____

_____

_____

_____

58. Are there any actions I regret taking when I was young? If I could go back now, what would I do differently? How would I try to change the outcome of my actions? While you may regret some actions during your lifetime, the fact you would do something differently now shows that you have grown, that is worth acknowledging.

_____

_____

_____

_____

_____

59. Are there any people I resent, or whose actions I resent from my childhood? Which people from my childhood do I feel wronged me in some way? In what ways have their actions impacted me?

_____

_____

_____

_____

_____

60. What emotions am I holding onto about these people and events? Why am I holding onto them, in what ways do they serve me?

_____

_____

_____

_____

_____

61. What does my inner child deserve to hear from these people? An apology? An admission of guilt? Nothing at all?

_____

_____

_____

_____

_____

62. How did I change my behaviour to adapt in these situations? Do I still employ these behaviours? Am I still living in survival mode?

_____

_____

_____

_____

_____

63. How can I change my current behaviour to reclaim my life? What actions can I implement to realign myself with the version of me that did not suffer through their actions?

_____

_____

_____

_____

_____

64. Do any things that remind me of unpleasant childhood memories still make me uncomfortable to this day? e.g., smells, sounds, subjects of conversation, any of which might evoke an unpleasant memory. Try to create as exhaustive a list as is possible.

_____

_____

_____

_____

_____

65. Go through your list from yesterday. Take a moment to consider each one, why does it provoke a reaction from you? What reaction is it? Does it make you feel unsafe, anger, grief? Remind yourself that you are safe now, or that while anger can be a useful tool at times it possibly no longer is of use to you here. Practice reminding yourself this with deep, calming breaths
when these thoughts are provoked again

_____

_____

_____

_____

_____

_____

_____

_____

_____

66. Unpleasant memories and emotions often manifest themselves physically, forcing us to acknowledge them. Where in your body can you feel the effects of any of your experiences? Do you feel like you are carrying around sadness or grief in your body?

_____

_____

_____

_____

67. Brainstorm ways you can help your body process and heal from your lived experiences. Maybe you need time to relax, or maybe you need to use up nervous energy, depending on what and how you feel the issue presents in your body. (Ideas: yoga, meditation, self-care evenings, running, etc.)

_____

_____

_____

_____

68. What do I grieve from my childhood? This can be as outright as the loss of a loved one, or it can be less tangible, like grieving the absence of what you deserved (i.e., the parents you deserved, the experience you deserved).

_____

_____

_____

_____

_____

69. How did you deal with this grief and how do you feel about it now? Are there times that amplify it? How do you cope with that reminder when it arises?

_____

_____

_____

_____

_____

70. Often it is easy to overlook sources of discomfort and disregard them. That is common with issues of parentification. In what ways did parentification affect you? In what ways were you required to grow up before you were ready?

_____

_____

_____

_____

_____

71. How does the impact of parentification still affect you? Has it changed the way you conduct yourself? What differences would there have been then and now if you hadn't experienced this?

_____

_____

_____

_____

72. What behaviours do you have that you would like to change, that stem from your childhood?

_____

_____

_____

_____

_____

_____

73. How can you work on changing them? What reminders or system can you create to do this? For example, if you want to change the way you react under pressure, perhaps the use of a grounding technique would help you stay in the present moment.

_____

_____

_____

_____

_____

74. What beliefs or thought patterns do you have that you would like to change, that stem from your childhood?

_____

_____

_____

_____

75. How can you work on changing them? In what ways can you interrupt these thoughts and challenge them, to adopt new beliefs that better serve you? For example, if you want to interrupt self-depreciating thoughts on your appearance, maybe focusing on a different feature you can genuinely compliment and stating it like an affirmation will slowly help you to associate seeing yourself with complimenting yourself instead of criticizing yourself.

_____

_____

_____

_____

Self reflection

76. If you have children, or may have them in the future, what do you want them to learn from you?

_____

_____

_____

_____

_____

77. How was your identity defined as a child? Did it resonate with you, or did it feel not quite right?

_____

_____

_____

_____

_____

78. How is your identity defined now? In what ways have you changed and grown in character?

_____

_____

_____

_____

_____

79. Who did you live with as a child and how has this shaped your view of family now?

_____

_____

_____

_____

_____

80. In what way have your childhood experiences shaped your values?

_____

_____

_____

_____

_____

_____

81. Who did your childhood self need?

_____

_____

_____

_____

_____

82. Who did your childhood self want to become?

_____

_____

_____

_____

_____

83. In what ways have you successfully become a person
your childhood self would be proud of?

_____

_____

_____

_____

_____

84. In what ways do you feel you could have done better?

_____

_____

_____

_____

_____

85. What do you think your childhood self would say, if they could see you now?

_____

_____

_____

_____

_____

Messages to others

This section is about what you would say to certain people if you could speak to them now and speak freely. This does not mean you have to say or send them anything, it is just for you. While you may also think of something quite lengthy, it can be as long or as short as you would like it to be. So, for the following prompts, think about what you would like to say to:

86. Your 5 year old self

87. Your 10 year old self

_____

_____

_____

_____

_____

_____

_____

_____

_____

_____

_____

_____

_____

_____

88. Your 15 year old self

_____

_____

_____

_____

_____

_____

_____

_____

_____

_____

_____

_____

_____

_____

89. Yourself today

_____

_____

_____

_____

_____

_____

_____

_____

_____

_____

_____

_____

_____

_____

90. Yourself in ten years

91. Your brother/sister

92. A childhood friend

93. A childhood teacher

94. Someone who hurt you

_____

_____

_____

_____

_____

_____

_____

_____

_____

_____

_____

_____

_____

_____

_____

95. Someone who betrayed you

_____

_____

_____

_____

_____

_____

_____

_____

_____

_____

_____

_____

_____

_____

96. Any future children you might have

_____

_____

_____

_____

_____

_____

_____

_____

_____

_____

_____

_____

_____

_____

Moving forward

97. I can forgive myself because...

_____

_____

_____

_____

_____

98. I can heal from this because...

_____

_____

_____

_____

_____

99. I love myself because...

_____

_____

_____

_____

_____

100. I can let go of things I do not need to hold onto anymore, I can decide now to let go of...

_____

_____

_____

_____

_____

101. I am grateful for...

_____

_____

_____

_____

_____

_____

Inner child affirmations

1. I am safe

2. I let go of the past, and I am thankful for the joy that is in my life now

3. I am excited to experience the joys the future has in store for me

4. I deserve to be loved, and I am loved

5. I love myself

6. I am thankful to myself for keeping myself safe

7. I deserve to enjoy my life

8. I am capable of healing

9. I amplify the abundance of joys in my life

10. I am proud of the person I have become, and excited to see how I will grow from here

What was one time you felt wronged as a child? Does this still affect you?

_____

_____

_____

_____

_____

_____

Think about a time where you have been betrayed. what would you say to that person now?

_____

_____

_____

_____

_____

what is one trait that you see in other people that you wish you had?

_____

_____

_____

_____

_____

_____

What triggers envy for you? why do you think this is?

_____

_____

_____

_____

_____

_____

Which behaviour that you know is wrong and has negative effects do you repeat over and over again?

_____

_____

_____

_____

_____

_____

How long do you reflect on failures or mistakes? do you struggle to forgive yourself? if yes, why?

_____

_____

_____

_____

_____

_____

are you honest with yourself about your feelings?

_____

_____

_____

_____

_____

_____

what makes you really angry and why?

_____

_____

_____

_____

_____

What was your childhood like? would you describe your childhood as happy?

_____

_____

_____

_____

_____

_____

have you forgiven all the people who ever hurt you?

_____

_____

_____

_____

_____

_____

what are you most afraid of? how does that fear hold you
back?

_____

_____

_____

_____

_____

_____

what emotions do you try to avoid feeling? what makes you
avoid them?

_____

_____

_____

_____

_____

what is something you should forgive yourself for? why haven't you forgiven yourself before? can you forgive yourself now?

_____

_____

_____

_____

_____

_____

what unhealthy attachments do you hold onto? (things, places, people) what fear do you have of ending these attachments?

_____

_____

_____

_____

_____

what grudge/incident are you holding on to? how can you let
this weight go?

_____

_____

_____

_____

_____

_____

how do you manage stress in your life? do you deal with
stress in a healthy or unhealthy way? how can you fix this?

_____

_____

_____

_____

_____

_____

what are your toxic traits? how do you project these onto others?

_____

_____

_____

_____

_____

_____

what is a toxic trait you have recognised in your parents? how did it make you feel when you realised this?

_____

_____

_____

_____

_____

_____

what aspects of yourself would you like to improve? why?

_____

_____

_____

_____

_____

_____

what is the biggest lie you have ever told yourself? why?

_____

_____

_____

_____

_____

_____

what would you say to your child self? your teenage self?

_____

_____

_____

_____

_____

_____

what are the words that you need to hear right now to feel
at peace?

_____

_____

_____

_____

_____

_____

what is one thing you wish others would know about you?

_____

_____

_____

_____

_____

_____

what is your biggest flaw? and what is your biggest
strength?

_____

_____

_____

_____

_____

where do you feel the safest? how do you comfort yourself?

_____

_____

_____

_____

_____

_____

what is getting in the way of you living the life you want?
how are you holding yourself back?

_____

_____

_____

_____

_____

_____

in what ways are you inauthentic? why?

_____

_____

_____

_____

_____

_____

have you ever badly hurt someone unintentionally? could
you have been kinder to them?

_____

_____

_____

_____

_____

in what ways are you hypocritical? do you break your own rules?

_____

_____

_____

_____

_____

_____

what are your bad habits? why don't you break them?

_____

_____

_____

_____

_____

_____

if you could get rid of one memory, which one would it be?
how would you be affected by no longer having this memory?

_____

_____

_____

_____

_____

_____

how easy or hard do you find asking for help when you need
it?

_____

_____

_____

_____

_____

_____

how would you like to be seen by those closest to you?

_____

_____

_____

_____

_____

_____

who do you consider to be your closest friend and why?

_____

_____

_____

_____

_____

_____

if you could relive one day of your life, what day would it be
and why?

_____

_____

_____

_____

_____

_____

how do you deal with emotional discomfort? what is your
outlet? do you have any addictions?

_____

_____

_____

_____

_____

how judged do you feel on a daily basis? how much of that judgement do you think is real? how much of it could you be imagining?

_____

_____

_____

_____

_____

_____

what do you hate about yourself and why?

_____

_____

_____

_____

_____

_____

how do you feel about the idea of love?

_____

_____

_____

_____

_____

_____

in what ways are you privileged? how often do you take
things for granted?

_____

_____

_____

_____

_____

have you ever made a promise to yourself and broken it? why?

_____

_____

_____

_____

_____

what irrational fears do you have? what sort of blocks do they cause?

_____

_____

_____

_____

_____

what can you declutter physically or emotionally to find
more ease and simplicity?

_____

_____

_____

_____

_____

_____

what is an accomplishment you are most proud of?

_____

_____

_____

_____

_____

_____

what is one of the most important lessons you have learned
through the years?

_____

_____

_____

_____

_____

are you surrounding yourself with people who bring out the
best in you? why do you keep them around?

_____

_____

_____

_____

_____

what would you be doing if money or other people's opinions
didn't hold you back?

_____

_____

_____

_____

_____

_____

what do you need to give up, say no to, or let go of?

_____

_____

_____

_____

_____

_____

what is something that other people do that annoys you? how does this reflect a part of yourself?

_____

_____

_____

_____

_____

_____

in what ways do you feel guilty? why?

_____

_____

_____

_____

_____

_____

how do you show up for others but fall short in showing up for yourself?

_____

_____

_____

_____

_____

_____

which of your weaknesses could also be seen as a strength?

_____

_____

_____

_____

_____

how worthy do you honestly believe you are?

_____

_____

_____

_____

_____

_____

do you find it easy or hard to trust people? why? could this
be considered a strength or weakness?

_____

_____

_____

_____

_____

which situations have shaped your personality and why?

_____

_____

_____

_____

_____

_____

when reflecting on your childhood what makes you extremely
angry or sad to this day?

_____

_____

_____

_____

_____

what parts of yourself do you suppress or deny?

_____

_____

_____

_____

_____

_____

what is your biggest struggle with loving yourself?

_____

_____

_____

_____

_____

_____

what is one compliment you struggle to accept about
yourself? why?

_____

_____

_____

_____

_____

_____

where in life do you need to slow down and take your time?

_____

_____

_____

_____

_____

are you in love with illusions and fantasies or truths and realities?

_____

_____

_____

_____

_____

_____

do you live mostly in the past, present or future? why?

_____

_____

_____

_____

_____

_____

are you afraid to be alone? if yes, what are you avoiding in yourself?

_____

_____

_____

_____

_____

_____

do you easily allow yourself to be happy? or does it take a lot to make you happy?

_____

_____

_____

_____

_____

do you tend to take on other people's burdens and pain?

_____

_____

_____

_____

_____

_____

what is the most important thing to you right now?

_____

_____

_____

_____

_____

_____

what is the root of your most recurring feeling?

_____

_____

_____

_____

_____

_____

what do you need less of in your life and why? what do you
need more of?

_____

_____

_____

_____

_____

do you listen more than you speak? are you present in life more often than absent?

_____

_____

_____

_____

_____

_____

is there a particularly traumatic event/situation that has occurred that you often think back to?

_____

_____

_____

_____

_____

what is one thing you look forward to every day?

_____

_____

_____

_____

_____

_____

what would make your younger self/teenage self proud of
you now?

_____

_____

_____

_____

_____

what does self love mean to you?

_____

_____

_____

_____

_____

_____

what is it about failure that scares you?

_____

_____

_____

_____

_____

_____

who is the loudest voice in your head and why? is that voice
negative or positive?

_____

_____

_____

_____

_____

_____

make a list of things you would do if you weren't afraid. How
would doing it impact your life?

_____

_____

_____

_____

_____

_____

what can you learn from your biggest triumph?

_____

_____

_____

_____

_____

_____

how aware of your thoughts, emotions and surroundings are
you during the day?

_____

_____

_____

_____

_____

how can you make more alone time for yourself and time to prioritise yourself?

_____

_____

_____

_____

_____

_____

are you confident within yourself or do you need others for validation? why? how can you change this?

_____

_____

_____

_____

_____

what lessons have pain, anger and sadness taught you?

_____

_____

_____

_____

_____

_____

if you died tomorrow would you feel as if you lived a
fulfilling life?

_____

_____

_____

_____

_____

how can you reframe the way you talk to yourself and be more confident?

_____

_____

_____

_____

_____

_____

what is a characteristic that makes you unique?

_____

_____

_____

_____

_____

what is something that you will never forget?

_____

_____

_____

_____

_____

_____

do you tend to blame your problems and failures on others?

_____

_____

_____

_____

_____

_____

how can you develop more motivation, inspiration and passion in your life?

_____

_____

_____

_____

_____

_____

do you take care of your body, as well as your mental and emotional needs?

_____

_____

_____

_____

_____

_____

how can you benefit from giving yourself more love?

_____

_____

_____

_____

_____

_____

what do you need to get off your chest today?

_____

_____

_____

_____

_____

_____

what is one area in your life you have grown in over the past few years? (health, relationships, finances, career, ect.)

_____

_____

_____

_____

_____

_____

what is your first thought when you open your eyes in the morning? are you happy with this?

_____

_____

_____

_____

_____

_____

are you pushing yourself to your fullest potential?

_____

_____

_____

_____

_____

_____

write about the last time you ran away from your
responsibilities. why did you do that? what were the results?

_____

_____

_____

_____

_____

_____

what do you need to start saying "yes" to?

_____

_____

_____

_____

_____

_____

share one of your most inner secrets, something you've never
told anyone.

_____

_____

_____

_____

_____

what needs to heal in your life right now?

_____

_____

_____

_____

_____

_____

what has made you a stronger person?

_____

_____

_____

_____

_____

_____

write yourself a letter accepting yourself for who you are.

_____

_____

_____

_____

_____

_____

what have you learned from this self discovery/ healing journey? write down some positive changes you are going to implement in your life.

_____

_____

_____

_____

_____

_____

Made in the USA
Monee, IL
19 October 2022

16187720R10066